BEN SETH-OLA

40 BIBLE THOUGHTS ON MARITAL FULFILMENT

Copyright © 2024 Ben Seyi-Ola

ISBN 979-8-9869061-8-8

All rights reserved. It is not legal to reproduce, duplicate, or transmit any part of this document, either electronically or in printed format. Recording of this publication is strictly prohibited, and any storage of this document is not allowed unless with written permission from the publisher, except for the use of brief quotations in a book review.

No patent liability is assumed with respect to the use of the information contained herein. Although every precaution has been taken in the preparation of this material, the author and the publisher assumes no responsibility for errors or omissions. Neither is any liability assumed for damages resulting from the use of the information contain herein.

CONTENTS

1. The Founder of Marriage..................7
2. Forgiveness in Marriage..................9
3. The Bliss Pause..................11
4. The power of Listening..................13
5. The Role of Trust..................15
6. The Importance of Boundaries..................17
7. Know Spouse's Needs..................19
8. Building emotional intimacy..................21
9. A Vital Component of Marriage..................23
10. Spending Quality Time..................25
11. Parenting Together..................27
12. Being best friend with your spouse..................29
13. Overcoming conflicts in Marriage..................31
14. The value of apologies..................33
15. Positive attitude in Marriage..................35
16. Maintaining individuality..................37
17. Dealing with Grief as a couple..................39
18. The Art of compromise in marriage..................41
19. The power of Prayer..................43
20. Building a strong support system..................45
21. The art of romance..................47
22. Dealing with Change..................49
23. Navigating cultural differences..................51
24. Keep your marriage exciting..................53
25. Family Devotion..................55

26.	The role of humor in marriage	57
27.	Overcoming infidelity	59
28.	Celebrating Milestones	61
29.	Keep Finding Joy and contentment	63
30.	The power of gratitude	65
31.	Benefits of Showing Appreciation	67
32.	Overcoming bitterness	69
33.	The role of counseling	71
34.	Building a strong marriage	73
35.	Family Dynamics with in-laws	75
36.	Supporting Each other	77
37.	Your relationship with God	79
38.	Serving the Lord together	81
39.	Establishing an enduring Marriage	83
40.	Living Out God's design	85

INTRODUCTION

Marriage is a significant relationship, and it should be a balance of fun and commitment. When considering whether to marry someone, think about activities you both enjoy doing together. For Christians, it's important to share certain goals and values. The most crucial aspect is both being committed to the Lord, which will help guide your home.

For Christian couples, God wants us to have a fulfilling and joyful marriage so that we can be at peace and raise children who are devoted to the Lord. When you have peace in your immediate family and a solid foundation in the knowledge of the Lord, certain issues will not arise in your family. That's because God is at the center of your home.

How do we build a home where God is at the center? How do we maintain a friendly atmosphere in our home consistently? How do we raise our children to love the Father? These are the questions we will answer in this book. I will also share how the level of communication and intimacy between couples is directly related to the warmth experienced in your home.

Please engage with every call to action and take the necessary steps to implement what is written in the book. You are on your way to building a home filled with love and happiness where everyone is heard and respected.

To make your home the best it can be, make sure you communicate with your partner and express your emotions. You will learn more about the commitment your home needs to be a standard Christian home. Your marriage can be a perfect example of a relationship ruled by God.

Let's begin.

Ben Seyi-Ola

1
THE FOUNDER OF MARRIAGE

Have you not read that He who created them from the beginning made them male and female, and said, 'For this reason a man shall leave his father and mother and be joined to his wife, and the two shall become one flesh'? So they are no longer two, but one flesh. What therefore God has joined together, let no man separate. **Matthew 19:4-6**

We cannot simply assume that marriage happens when two people fall in love on their own. We must reflect on the very beginning when God created man and arranged for Adam and Eve to marry. Therefore, we understand that marriage is both a human and divine institution. When a man and a woman marry, they come together in a way that symbolizes harmony, love, and unity.

As Christians who understand God's intention and plan, we have a responsibility to uphold the sanctity of marriage and support those who are married. Our respect for marriage should stem from the knowledge that God instituted it.

We should set a good example for others through our actions. When people look at married couples, they should see the love and unity between Christ and the church. God designed marriage to be a lifelong relationship where spouses rely on God for support and provision, and serve as helpers, confidants, and friends to one another. It is also essential to embody the values of love, devotion, and self-sacrifice that are at the core of a successful marriage.

Call to action: Have you been failing to honor your marriage? Remember, marriage is an institution by God, it is sacred.

2
FORGIVENESS IN MARRIAGE

Bear with each other and forgive one another if any of you has a grievance against someone. Forgive as the Lord forgave you. **Colossians 3:13**

Forgiveness is essential for a happy and successful marriage. As imperfect human beings, we make mistakes and sometimes hurt our spouse unintentionally. However, forgiveness helps us overcome our flaws and deepen our bond as a couple.

Living together as husband and wife means spending more time with each other than anyone else in this world. It also means becoming more vulnerable and open with each other, which can lead to both freedom and disrespect if not handled properly. Hence, forgiveness is crucial in any marriage to avoid resentment and revenge.

The Bible teaches us extensively about forgiveness and emphasizes its significance in reflecting God's forgiveness towards us. As believers, we are encouraged to emulate God's character and show kindness and empathy towards our partner, just as God has done for us. We should be patient with one another, accept responsibility for our own shortcomings, and apologize when we have wronged our spouse.

In Colossians 3:13, we are reminded to forgive each other as the Lord forgave us. Ephesians 4:32 encourages us to be kind to one another, tenderhearted, and forgiving, just as God in Christ forgave us.

Therefore, it's important to talk openly and honestly with your spouse about any unresolved issues in your marriage. Don't let resentment build up, instead, try to work things out by communicating and extending forgiveness. Remember, forgiveness is essential for a godly home.

Call to action: If you have any unresolved issues with your spouse, take the time to talk it out and hug it out. Practice forgiveness and let God's love guide your marriage.

3

BLISS PAUSE

God is our refuge and strength, a very present help in trouble. **Psalm 46:1**

Marriage is a beautiful institution established by God from the beginning of creation. This long-term vow between a husband and wife should be marked by fondness, esteem, and mutual obedience.

However, in this fallen world, marriages often face various crises such as financial difficulties, infidelity, communication breakdown, and domestic violence. These challenges can make it easy to feel overwhelmed, hopeless, and even consider giving up on the marriage.

Even though there are some issues that a Christian family may never experience because of their knowledge of God, they may still face what is called a "bliss pause." For example, after going on vacation together, a couple may get into a funny argument due to something that just happened.

This can lead to a heated or smooth argument, and at this point, there is a "bliss pause," where it may seem like they never had a sweet relationship.

It's essential to remember that God is your help, especially when you are both annoyed with each other. Instead of going back and forth in your argument, take a moment to pray. It's even better if you both pray together. This will help you both come back from the place of prayer with a peaceful mind, which is expected of you. Remember to share your problems with God, and make praying for your marriage and family a normal thing during your prayer time. God who brought you together is with you all the way.

Call to action: Make praying to God an essential part of your marriage to overcome challenges and experience peace.

4
THE POWER OF LISTENING

My dear brothers and sisters, take note of this: Everyone should be quick to listen, slow to speak, and slow to become angry. **James 1:19**

When someone approaches you to talk, what do you believe they need at that precise moment? They require a sympathetic ear. Nothing compares to having someone listen to you when you share your thoughts.

If couples would just listen to each other, many relationships and marriages wouldn't go through unstable periods. Sometimes, your spouse's reaction may result from you not listening to them. Be the less busy spouse when your partner wants to talk to you. Do not attempt to listen while not paying attention. Some of us even listen to what's being said while using our phones.

Listening has the power to change relationships, create trust, and promote understanding. The

Bible stresses the value of listening in numerous verses, including James 1:19, which says, "*My dear brothers and sisters, take note of this: Everyone should be quick to listen, slow to speak and slow to become angry.*"

By paying attention to others, we show them our respect for their ideas and emotions. We give them our undivided attention and provide a safe space for them to express themselves. This can result in deeper connections, improved communication, and ultimately stronger relationships.

Listening not only fosters relationships but also promotes learning and development. Proverbs 19:20 says, "*Listen to advice and accept discipline, and at the end, you will be counted among the wise.*" By listening to others, we expose ourselves to new viewpoints and ideas, develop greater empathy and comprehension, and make it easier for us to deal with difficult circumstances.

Call to action: We must be intentional about giving our full attention to listening to those who speak with us.

5
THE ROLE OF TRUST

Trust in the Lord with all your heart and lean not on your own understanding; in all your ways submit to him, and he will make your paths straight. **Proverbs 3:5-6**

All healthy relationships, whether they are between friends, family, or romantic partners, must begin and end with trust. Trust means having faith that someone or something will act in our best interests. When we trust someone, we are prepared to share our vulnerabilities with them, exposing ourselves to the risk of suffering harm. Once trust is fractured, it can be difficult to fix and could even devastate the relationship beyond redemption.

Just as trust is critical in human relationships, it is also crucial in our relationship with God. Depending on the situation, trust may be the only thing that keeps our relationship with God going.

In our personal relationships, we may learn certain things about our partner or their job that concern us. Perhaps our partner has been too busy to share these things with us. Maybe others start telling us strange things about our partner. However, because we trust our spouse and have faith in them, we do not need to see evidence to defend them.

But we should not only trust our spouse because we have determined that they are trustworthy. We should trust our partner because God's power operates through them. Not just anyone can have a significant impact on our lives. The Bible has an impact on our lives because it helps us develop admirable character. The word of God should be our primary influence.

Call to action: If something is unclear to you, ask questions. Do not assume. A relationship built on trust is better than one without trust. Take active steps to clear doubts in your heart about your spouse.

6
THE IMPORTANCE OF BOUNDARIES

Like a city whose walls are broken through is a person who lacks self-control. **Proverbs 25:28**

In any relationship, including a marriage, establishing and maintaining healthy levels of intimacy, communication, and respect requires setting boundaries. Unfortunately, the word "boundaries" has often been misunderstood as negative. However, the context in which we use the term is crucial.

In a marriage, setting limits on behavior and communication is essential to maintain a happy and fulfilling relationship. We must respect the needs and desires of our spouse while also being clear about our own. Healthy boundaries enable us to create an environment where intimacy and vulnerability can flourish.

Moreover, boundaries in a marriage can prevent disputes and misunderstandings. By clearly communicating our expectations and what is not acceptable, we are less likely to feel hurt or resentment when our boundaries are crossed. This promotes trust and strengthens the foundation of our marriage.

As believers, it is our responsibility to set limits that align with God's Word and His purposes for our lives. Setting boundaries based on love, respect, and honor for our spouse and ourselves is necessary to achieve this. It also means being prepared to show mercy and forgiveness when those boundaries are crossed and working together to find a solution.

When setting boundaries, we should focus on giving our spouse the best version of ourselves. We need to ask ourselves if there are things we need to communicate about our strengths and limitations to our spouse to establish healthy boundaries.

Call to Action: Take some time to reflect on your relationship with your spouse. Are there things you need to communicate to establish healthy boundaries? Remember that setting boundaries is essential to knowing what to expect from each other and creating a happy and fulfilling marriage.

7
KNOW YOUR SPOUSE'S NEEDS

However, each one of you also must love his wife as he loves himself, and the wife must respect her husband.
Ephesians 5:33

Expressing and comprehending each other's needs can lead to a harmonious relationship. You should be aware of both your and your spouse's expectations.

For example, imagine you want to honor your wife on her birthday. You leave work early to buy her some presents. She's excited when you give her the gift, but as she opens it, her smile fades.

What do you think happened?

Part of loving your spouse is understanding their preferences and needs. This means doing your research and asking important questions.

Some people value hugs the most during difficult

times, while others prefer a pat on the back. What do you prefer?

After a tough day, how do you want your spouse to comfort you? Would you like a cuddle, or would you prefer for them to hold your hand?

Instead of assuming that our spouses already know these things, we should talk to them about it. Making assumptions can lead to bigger problems down the line.

When we handle things properly and clear up misunderstandings, we realize that our expectations are reasonable. We don't have to strain our brains trying to predict what kind of coffee our spouse wants in the afternoon.

Call to Action: Have deep conversations with your spouse. It'll lead to a smoother relationship journey without any hiccups. Don't forget to show love and respect, as the Bible teaches us.

8
BUILDING EMOTIONAL INTIMACY

A new command I give you: Love one another. As I have loved you, so you must love one another. ***John 13:34***

I have witnessed many individuals terminate friendships that had lasted for ten years or more. Reflecting on what occurred in the relationship, it becomes apparent that there was insufficient consistency to sustain it.

When two people first meet and develop a bond, they both invest effort into maintaining the connection by calling, chatting, and taking various actions. When they stop putting in the same amount of effort, the relationship suffers.

The journey doesn't conclude when you court and marry your spouse. You must continue to make a conscious effort, just as you did before, to maintain what you have now that you are a unit.

As a married individual with children, I am familiar with how marriage works and what happens when children enter the picture. The newborn baby becomes the center of attention, and sometimes we lose track of ourselves in the process. We forget who we are and how we came to possess this bundle of joy.

Then, we immerse ourselves in the nursery and the first stages of our children's lives, losing sight of the fact that we were first a couple before we became parents. Being excellent parents is fantastic, but it shouldn't be our sole objective. Every aspect of our lives can thrive. Remember to take care of yourself so that you can continue to work well together and succeed in other areas as your relationship grows and thrives. Whether it's a special day or an ordinary day, show your partner you care with a thoughtful and surprising present.

Call to Action: When was the last time you went on a special date for just you and your spouse?

9
A VITAL COMPONENT OF MARRIAGE

The husband should fulfill his marital duty to his wife, and likewise the wife to her husband. The wife does not have authority over her own body but yields it to her husband. In the same way, the husband does not have authority over his own body but yields it to his wife. **1 Corinthians 7:3-4**

Sexual intimacy is a vital aspect of a fulfilling marriage according to the Bible. It is seen as a holy and beautiful gift from God to be enjoyed within the bounds of marriage. In order to cultivate sexual intimacy, we must prioritize communication and empathy in our relationship. This involves both expressing our own preferences and actively listening to our spouse's needs. It also means prioritizing our physical and mental well-being, as these factors greatly impact our sexual satisfaction.

Creating space for intimacy is also crucial. This may mean scheduling date nights, planning romantic getaways, or simply spending quality time together. As followers of Christ, it's vital to seek God's counsel and direction in all aspects of our marriage, including our sexual relations. If necessary, it's also important to seek the help of a professional or counselor.

By prioritizing communication, empathy, and intimacy, we can honor and serve our spouse while enjoying the gift of sexual intimacy within marriage.

Call to Action: Be open with your spouse and learn to communicate freely about any issues related to your sexual relationship.

10
SPENDING QUALITY TIME

Two are better than one, because they have a good return for their labor: If either of them falls down, one can help the other up. But pity anyone who falls and has no one to help them up. ***Ecclesiastes 4:9-10***

The commitment of spending quality time together is one of the most crucial elements in building a successful marriage. Investing time in your relationship promotes effective communication, intimacy, and trust between partners. A healthy and prosperous marriage requires quality time, which involves making your spouse feel valued and appreciated.

The above passage highlights the significance of companionship and cooperation in a marriage. When two people prioritize each other, they establish a strong bond that is difficult to break.

It is recommended that couples prioritize spending quality time together in their marriage.

This can include setting aside time for a monthly weekend getaway or a weekly date night. Put away your phones and work to focus on each other. Engage in new hobbies or activities together to create shared experiences.

Inquiring with open-mindedness and being attentive to your partner can enhance your communication abilities. Keep in mind that the quality of time spent together matters more than the quantity. Even brief interactions throughout the day can have a significant impact.

Investing in your relationship will strengthen the bond between you and your spouse, enabling you to overcome any adversity. The teachings of Ecclesiastes emphasize the importance of prioritizing your spouse. Making a conscious effort to spend quality time with your partner will undoubtedly strengthen your marriage.

Call to Action: Are you prioritizing quality time with your spouse? If not, it's time to start making this a priority in your marriage.

11
PARENTING TOGETHER

Train up a child in the way he should go, and when he is old he will not depart from it. ***Proverbs 22:6***

A marriage can bring great happiness and fulfillment through the parenting journey. Couples who decide to have children together can work towards a common goal and build a family that reflects their values and worldview. However, parenting can also present its own set of challenges, and it's crucial for couples to collaborate and overcome these difficulties to create a solid and satisfying family life.

The importance of co-parenting is well-explained in the Bible. Prioritizing family and parenting is crucial. This means effective communication about parenting choices and teamwork to develop a unified parenting strategy. It also involves scheduling family time and creating opportunities for shared experiences. To raise kids with a positive example of a happy marriage, it means setting an example of a loving and healthy relationship.

A successful marriage must include cooperative parenting. Couples can build a solid and devoted family that upholds their values and beliefs by intentionally raising children together. When it comes to parenting with a purpose, remember the teachings of Proverbs and Ephesians, and make a vow to prioritize parenting together in your marriage.

You and your spouse need to present a united front on all issues, including the proper method of reprimand or punishment. It's important to agree on a consistent approach so your kids don't think that one parent is more lenient than the other.

Call to Action: Take time to discuss and agree upon a consistent approach to training and disciplining your children.

12
BEING BEST FRIEND WITH YOUR SPOUSE

A friend loves at all times, and a brother is born for a time of adversity. ***Proverbs 17:17***

Some people marry their childhood friends and go on to have children together, while others meet their partners recently before getting married. Regardless of how our love story began, it's wonderful that my spouse and I are best friends.

One of the benefits of marriage is having your spouse as your best friend, someone you can confide in, trust, and share your joys and sorrows with. Developing a friendship with your spouse not only brings rewards but also paves the way for a happy and fulfilling marriage.

The value of love and loyalty in friendship cannot be overstated. During difficult times, a friend can be a source of comfort. Allowing your spouse to become a trusted best friend and confidant will benefit your marriage and relationship.

Making your spouse's friendship a top priority involves setting aside time for deeper communication, sharing interests and pastimes, and having fun together. It also means trying to communicate with your partner and give them your full attention. By regularly making time for each other, such as a weekly date night or daily check-ins, couples can work on developing their friendship.

Being best friends with your spouse can be humorous at times, like wanting to complain about your partner to your best friend. However, it can also be fun because of this.

Call to Action: By building a strong foundation of love, loyalty, and companionship, couples can weather any storm and create a joyful and lasting partnership. Build on this foundation.

13
OVERCOMING CONFLICTS IN MARRIAGE

Bear with each other and forgive one another if any of you has a grievance against someone. Forgive as the Lord forgave you. **Colossians 3:13**

Every relationship, including marriage, is bound to face conflicts at some point. While conflicts can be challenging, they also present opportunities for growth and learning. Resolving disputes amicably can foster intimacy and strengthen the bond between partners. When facing challenges in their relationship, it is crucial for spouses to demonstrate tolerance, empathy, and a resolve to collaborate in finding solutions. The Bible emphasizes the value of reconciliation and forgiveness in relationships (Ephesians 4:32).

Couples should prioritize resolving disputes together by actively listening to one another, handling disagreements with compromise and forgiveness, and expressing their feelings in a healthy way. It's also important to make time to talk about problems and be willing to seek outside help if needed. Active listening strategies, such as restating their partner's perspective, empathy, and understanding, can help couples work towards conflict resolution (James 1:19).

Disagreements and problems are inevitable in any relationship, but what matters is how we respond to them and treat one another. We cannot respond like unbelievers when conflicts arise. Instead, we should show what we've learned and know at this time. Forgiveness is crucial to the success of any relationship, so we must be willing to forgive (Colossians 3:13).

Couples can strengthen their bond and increase intimacy by following the guidance of the Bible and committing to resolving differences together.

Call to Action: Remember the importance of forgiveness and communication when it comes to overcoming conflicts in marriage, and make a commitment to working through challenges together.

14
THE VALUE OF APOLOGIES

Therefore, if you are offering your gift at the altar and there remember that your brother or sister has something against you, leave your gift there in front of the altar. First go and be reconciled to them; then come and offer your gift. **Matthew 5:23-24**

In any healthy relationship, including marriage, it's essential to include apologies. Apologies demonstrate humility, compassion, and a preparedness to own up to one's mistakes. When apologies are offered and accepted, they can lead to relationship healing and reconciliation. In marriage, making amends is crucial to maintaining a strong and satisfying union.

The passage above highlights the importance of seeking reconciliation and making amends with others before presenting gifts or worship to God. If you're holding a grudge against someone, be patient with them and extend forgiveness. Forgive others as the Lord forgave you. Forgiveness means completely putting past wrongs behind us.

Forgiving is critical because it provides a pathway for healing and restoring relationships. In a couple's marriage, apologizing should be a top priority.

Learn to sincerely apologize when you're in the wrong. This means being ready to acknowledge your mistakes, express regret, and make amends. It also means being ready to forgive your spouse and accept their apologies. Couples can practice giving and accepting apologies by engaging in active listening exercises, recognizing their roles in conflicts, and showing empathy and understanding.

A marriage cannot be happy and successful without readiness to make amends. By following the guidance of the Bible and prioritizing apologies and forgiveness, couples can maintain a strong and loving relationship.

Call to Action: Remember the importance of seeking reconciliation and making amends when conflicts arise. Try to apologize sincerely and forgive others as the Lord forgave you.

15
POSITIVE ATTITUDE IN MARRIAGE

Finally, brothers and sisters, whatever is true, whatever is noble, whatever is right, whatever is pure, whatever is lovely, whatever is admirable—if anything is excellent or praiseworthy—think about such things. ***Philippians 4:8***

Maintaining a positive attitude in marriage is essential to creating a happy and fulfilling relationship. A positive attitude can foster love, respect, and appreciation for your spouse, helping you navigate through difficult times with grace and optimism. When both partners maintain a positive attitude, they can create a sense of unity and build a strong foundation for their marriage.

To prioritize maintaining a positive attitude in your marriage, focus on the good in your spouse and relationship, express gratitude and appreciation for one another, and find joy and humor in everyday life. Additionally, be willing to forgive and move on from negative experiences, and choose to see challenges as opportunities for growth and learning. Couples can work on maintaining a positive attitude by practicing gratitude and appreciation, positive self-talk, and making a conscious effort to focus on the good in their relationship.

Communication is also vital in a marriage, so make sure to communicate regularly and openly with your spouse, and be willing to compromise and work through challenges together. By following the wisdom of the Bible and choosing to focus on the good in your spouse and relationship, you can create a sense of unity and build a strong foundation for your marriage.

Call to Action: Remember to practice gratitude and appreciation, communicate openly, and be willing to work through challenges together.

16
MAINTAINING INDIVIDUALITY

Each of you should use whatever gift you have received to serve others, as faithful stewards of God's grace in its various forms. **1 Peter 4:10**

Maintaining your own unique identity while building a strong marriage is crucial to creating a healthy and fulfilling relationship. While marriage involves forming a strong partnership and sense of unity, it is also important for each partner to maintain their own interests, values, and sense of self.

When both partners can maintain their individuality, they can bring diverse perspectives and strengths to their relationship and create a stronger sense of mutual respect and appreciation. This passage emphasizes the importance of using our individual gifts and talents to serve others and make a positive impact on the world.

Couples should prioritize maintaining their individuality while building a strong marriage.

This means encouraging each other's interests and hobbies, respecting each other's values and beliefs, and making time for personal growth and self-care. It also means being willing to compromise and find a balance between individual needs and the needs of the relationship.

Couples can work on maintaining their individuality by setting aside time for personal hobbies and interests, pursuing individual goals and dreams, and communicating openly and honestly about their needs and desires.

It is also important to celebrate each other's accomplishments and strengths, and to support each other through challenges and setbacks. By following the wisdom of the Bible and using our unique gifts and talents to serve others, couples can bring a sense of mutual respect and appreciation to their relationship.

Call to Action: Remember to prioritize personal growth and self-care, communicate openly and honestly, and find a balance between individual needs and the needs of the relationship.

17
DEALING WITH PAIN TOGETHER AS A COUPLE

Praise be to the God and Father of our Lord Jesus Christ, the Father of compassion and the God of all comfort, who comforts us in all our troubles, so that we can comfort those in any trouble with the comfort we ourselves receive from God. ***2 Corinthians 1:3-4***

Supporting each other through the grieving process as a couple is a difficult but important aspect of marriage. Whether it is the loss of a loved one, a job, or a dream, grieving together can help couples feel supported and help them navigate through difficult times with understanding. It is important for couples to acknowledge and validate each other's emotions, and to work together to find healthy ways to cope with grief and loss. This passage emphasizes the importance of finding comfort in God's love and using that comfort to support and comfort others who are going through difficult times.

Couples must prioritize supporting each other through grief and loss. This means acknowledging and validating each other's emotions, being willing to listen and provide comfort, and finding healthy ways to cope together. It also means being willing to seek outside support, such as therapy or support groups, if needed. Couples can work on coping with grief and loss by practicing open and honest communication, finding healthy ways to express emotions, and finding ways to honor and remember what has been lost. They may prioritize self-care by setting aside some time for themselves or seek support from friends, family, or a faith community.

By following the wisdom of the Bible, including verses such as Psalm 34:18 which states, "The Lord is close to the brokenhearted and saves those who are crushed in spirit," couples can support each other through difficult times and come out stronger on the other side.

Call to action: If you are experiencing grief and loss as a couple, remember to prioritize open communication, find healthy ways to cope together, and seek support when needed.

18
THE ART OF COMPROMISE IN MARRIAGE

Do nothing out of selfish ambition or vain conceit. Rather, in humility value others above yourselves, not looking to your own interests but each of you to the interests of the others.
Philippians 2:3-4

Compromise is essential to creating a strong and happy marriage. The goal of compromise is to find a middle ground that meets everyone's needs while promoting mutual respect and growth. Learning to compromise can help couples navigate conflicts and difficulties more effectively, while building a sense of cohesion and understanding.

Prioritizing compromise is crucial in a relationship. This involves finding common ground, being willing to compromise for the sake of the relationship, and listening to each other's viewpoints. It also requires developing empathy and putting ourselves in our partner's shoes.

Couples can improve their ability to compromise by engaging in active listening exercises, expressing themselves clearly and politely, and being open to finding unique solutions that meet both partners' needs. It's important to understand that reaching a compromise is a process that requires patience, adaptability, and a willingness to improve.

Remember, partnership is the implication of marriage. It's not always necessary to make all the final decisions. Occasionally, you need to make room for your partner's wishes.

Couples can develop a sense of unity and understanding that enhances their relationship by prioritizing their partner's needs and following the guidance of the Bible. If you put your partner first and your partner does the same for you, you can create a stronger bond.

Call to Action: Make sure to give active listening and clear, respectful expression a high priority. Be willing to find creative solutions that meet both partners' needs.

19
THE POWER OF PRAYER

Therefore confess your sins to each other and pray for each other so that you may be healed. The prayer of a righteous person is powerful and effective. **James 5:16**

A vital aspect of building a strong and successful marriage is the power of prayer. When couples pray together, they develop stronger bonds with each other, draw closer to God, and find more support and guidance during difficult times. Prayer allows couples to experience God's comforting presence, hope, and peace.

This passage emphasizes the importance of confessing our sins and praying for one another because we know that our prayers can be powerful and effective. Couples should prioritize prayer in their relationship by making time for group prayer, discussing their hopes and concerns, and imploring God for help and guidance. It is also crucial to listen attentively when your partner prays and to support and encourage them.

Making it a practice to pray daily can help couples improve the effectiveness of their prayers. This can be achieved by saying grace before meals, in the morning or evening, or at bedtime. It is vital to be honest and straightforward in your prayers, expressing your deepest worries and requesting God's guidance and assistance.

Couples can also seek support from their faith community in addition to praying together. This can involve attending church together, joining a prayer group, or seeking help from a therapist who shares their faith. By prioritizing prayer in their relationship and adhering to biblical wisdom, couples can deepen their relationship with God.

Call to Action: Remember to make time for prayer together, be honest and open in your prayers, and seek support from your faith community. Always ensure that any cited Bible verses are accurate.

20
BUILDING A STRONG SUPPORT SYSTEM

Two are better than one, because they have a good return for their labor: If either of them falls down, one can help the other up. But pity anyone who falls and has no one to help them up." ***Ecclesiastes 4:9***

Developing a sturdy support network is necessary for a happy and successful marriage. It establishes a foundation of love, trust, and support between partners, enabling them to navigate difficulties and overcome obstacles together.

Think of a couple attempting to lift a large object. Together, they can lift it effortlessly and painlessly. If they try to lift it by themselves, they might struggle or hurt themselves. Similarly, couples with a strong support system are better able to overcome difficulties and obstacles in their marriage.

Building a strong support system should be a priority for couples. This involves deliberately fostering ties with relatives, friends, and other couples who share their values and can offer moral and practical support. Reaching out to friends and family, joining a social or religious organization, or attending counseling or support groups are all ways that couples can strengthen their network of friends and family.

Along with actively working to forge connections and foster a sense of community, it is crucial to be open and honest with your partner about your needs for support. Couples can also look for tools to improve their communication and better understand each other's needs and desires, such as books or counseling. By adhering to the guidance of the Bible and placing a priority on their relationships and community, couples can navigate difficulties more easily.

Call to Action: Remember to be intentional about cultivating relationships with family, friends, and other couples to build a strong support system for your marriage.

21
THE ART OF ROMANCE

Let him kiss me with the kisses of his mouth! For your love is better than wine; your anointing oils are fragrant; your name is oil poured out; therefore virgins love you. Draw me after you; let us run. The king has brought me into his chambers. **Song of Solomon 1:2-4**

Romance is a crucial component of any successful marriage. It fosters closer relationships, helps people stay connected, and uplifts daily life.

Think of a garden that's been lovingly and attentively maintained. The fruits are plentiful, and the flowers are fully blossomed. When couples prioritize the romantic arts in their marriage, their union can flourish and grow, bringing happiness and fulfillment to both partners.

It's important for partners to prioritize romance in their marriage. This means making intentional efforts to create moments of intimacy and connection, even amidst daily stress. It can be as simple as a casual date, a romantic surprise, or a small act of kindness. Expressions of physical affection, like holding hands and embracing are essential for fostering romance. To maintain the romance, it's critical to be open and honest with each other about your needs and wants, and be willing to try new things.

To deepen emotional connection and enhance their awareness of each other's needs and longings., couples can turn to resources like books or counseling. By adhering to biblical guidance and placing a high value on intimacy and connection, couples can nurture their relationship and grow closer.

Call to Action: Remember to be intentional about creating moments of romance, prioritize physical touch, and communicate openly and honestly.

22
DEALING WITH CHANGE

To everything there is a season, A time for every purpose under heaven. **Ecclesiastes 3:1 NKJV**

There is a time for everything and that seasons of change are a part of God's plan.

It's important to remember that change is an inevitable part of life, and it can impact every aspect of our lives, including our marriages. Whether it's a change in career, health, or family dynamics, adapting to change can be challenging for couples. However, the Bible provides wisdom and guidance on how to navigate through these changes.

Think of a couple on a boat journeying through choppy waters. The waves are unpredictable, and the winds are strong, but the couple works together to navigate through the challenges and emerge on the other side, stronger and more united. Similarly, in marriage, couples can face change as a team, supporting and encouraging each other through the transitions.

Couples are urged to tackle change with an optimistic mindset and a flexibility to adapt. This means being open to new opportunities and experiences, communicating openly and honestly with each other, and seeking out support when needed.

Couples can also proactively prepare for changes by discussing potential challenges and developing strategies to manage them together. It is essential to listen to each other's concerns and to work together to find solutions that are mutually beneficial.

Call to Action: Gain courage from your faith by looking to God for guidance through prayer and reflecting on the wisdom found in biblical teachings. Through prayer, couples can find comfort and strength in knowing that God is with them through every season of life.

23
NAVIGATING CULTURAL DIFFERENCES

There is neither Jew nor Greek, there is neither slave nor free, there is neither male nor female; for you are all one in Christ Jesus. **Galatians 3:28**

Navigating cultural differences in marriage can be challenging, but it can also be an opportunity for growth and learning. Couples should approach cultural differences with curiosity and respect. This means being open to learning about each other's cultural backgrounds, asking questions, and actively listening to each other's perspectives.

Couples can also find ways to incorporate each other's cultures into their daily lives, whether it's through food, music, or celebrations. By embracing each other's cultures, couples can create a rich and diverse family culture that reflects both of their backgrounds.

Imagine a couple from different cultural backgrounds sharing a meal together. They each bring their unique dishes and relate experiences of their cultural practices. This experience helps them to discover more about each other's backgrounds and develop a deeper appreciation for each other's cultures. In the same way, couples can embrace their cultural differences and learn from each other's unique perspectives.

It is also important for couples to communicate openly and honestly about their cultural differences and to seek out support when needed. This could mean seeking out a counselor or mentor who has experience working with couples from diverse cultural backgrounds.

In addition, couples can draw strength from their faith by turning to God for guidance and wisdom. The Bible provides examples of couples from different cultural backgrounds who worked through their differences with God's help, such as Ruth and Boaz (Ruth 2-4).

Call to Action: Couples should approach cultural differences with curiosity and respect, not as obstacles, but as opportunities for growth and learning.

24
KEEP YOUR MARRIAGE FRESH AND EXCITING

Let your fountain be blessed, and rejoice with the wife of your youth. **Proverbs 5:18-19**

To keep your marriage fulfilling, it's critical to sustain interest and excitement. The Bible encourages us to be joyful in our spouse and to always cherish being with them.

Making quality time for each other and trying new things together are crucial for couples. This can involve exploring new hobbies, places, or restaurants. Couples can keep the spark in their relationship alive by engaging in fun and novel activities together.

For instance, consider a couple who plans a surprise date night every month. One month, the husband arranges a nighttime picnic, while the wife sets up a couple's massage for the following month. They continue to enjoy each other's company by keeping their relationship exciting and surprising each other.

It's vital to continue pursuing each other physically and emotionally. This involves prioritizing intimacy in the relationship and improving the depth of the relationship This may involve scheduling time for meaningful conversations, prioritizing physical touch, and regularly expressing gratitude and appreciation for one another.

Couples can also benefit from seeking tools and guidance to improve their marriage. This may involve attending marriage seminars or counseling sessions, reading books about marriage together, or seeking advice from trusted mentors or married couples. As it says in Proverbs 15:22, "Plans fail for lack of counsel, but with many advisers, they succeed."

Call to Action: Let's follow the guidance of the Bible in loving and honoring our spouses, and making our relationships a top priority in our lives.

25

FAMILY DEVOTION

And these words which I command you today shall be in your heart. You shall teach them diligently to your children, and shall talk of them when you sit in your house, when you walk by the way, when you lie down, and when rise up.
Deuteronomy 6:6-7

It is important to prioritize and incorporate family devotions into your daily schedule. This includes setting aside time each day for your family to read the Bible together, pray together, and discuss what was read. To make it more engaging for kids, you can use kid-friendly Bibles, videos, or songs.

Imagine a family reading a passage from the Bible together and discussing it each night before dinner. They take turns leading the devotion and expounding on the passage as they do so. By consistently prioritizing family devotions, they deepen their understanding of God's word and build stronger bonds with one another.

Family devotions are not only important for children but can also improve relationships between spouses. Couples can strengthen their spiritual bond and develop their relationship with God by discussing their beliefs and sharing their faith with each other.

To strengthen your family's faith, consider seeking resources and assistance from small-group Bible studies, church services, and other events. You can also get advice from reputable pastors or other Christian families.

As you strive to raise your family in the faith, seek inspiration and direction from the Bible. Remember that it provides wisdom on how to love and care for your families, how to raise children in a godly way, and how to prioritize your relationships with God above all else.

Call to Action: Make family devotions a priority in your daily schedule and seek out resources and assistance to strengthen your family's faith. Let the Bible guide and inspire you in your efforts to raise your family in the faith.

26
THE ROLE OF HUMOR IN MARRIAGE

A joyful heart is good medicine, but a crushed spirit dries up the bones. **Proverbs 17:22**

When you enter some homes, you may notice a warm and joyful atmosphere. One thing you may notice is that there's someone in the house who acts as a comedian, making people laugh and smile. This is a result of the household's strong sense of humor.

Humor can play a vital role in creating and maintaining a healthy and happy marriage. It promotes a sense of playfulness and connection between spouses, helps to ease tension, and brings joy.

Imagine a couple who regularly incorporate humor into their interactions - whether it's through telling jokes, watching comedies together, or playful teasing. By embracing humor, they foster a spirit of joy and lightheartedness, which helps to strengthen their bond and build resilience under pressure.

It's recommended that couples actively seek out humorous moments in their interactions. This can involve trying to joke around, tell amusing stories, or interact in a lighthearted manner. Incorporating humor into daily activities or routines can also mean singing silly songs while cooking or engaging in playful activities during long car rides.

It's important to keep in mind that humor should always be used to lift and bring joy, never to minimize or demean your spouse. Couples should also be mindful of each other's sense of humor and avoid making hurtful or offensive jokes or remarks.

Spending time together and regularly laughing can also benefit couples. This could involve planning fun activities, setting aside time to relax, or simply enjoying each other's company in the present.

Call to Action: How can you bring more joy and humor into your home? Take steps to cultivate a friendly and cheerful ambiance for yourself and your spouse.

27
OVERCOMING INFIDELITY

Trust in the Lord with all your heart and lean not on your own understanding; in all your ways submit to him, and he will make your paths straight. ***Proverbs 3:5-6***

With the help of God, re-establishing trust and healing a relationship is feasible following infidelity in a marriage. Even when the person you love the most hurts you, it is important to remain faithful. As a believer, forgiveness should be your default attitude, regardless of the nature of the offense.

Consider a couple who has experienced the devastation of adultery. The betrayed spouse may feel overwhelmed with anger, betrayal, and grief. However, with God's assistance, they can begin the healing process. This may include going to counseling, being open and honest with one another, and taking measures to rebuild trust.

Couples must embrace the healing and restoration process, which may involve addressing the infidelity and the challenging feelings that come with it. It is important to approach these discussions in a respectful and loving manner. Couples should also be willing to seek advice and support from dependable friends, family members, or professionals.

Forgiveness is crucial to the healing process. As the Bible commands, we must learn to put up with one another and forgive one another. We forgive because we are aware that God has already pardoned us, and we should show mercy to others just as it has been shown to us.

The world may not expect you to forgive and move on from situations like infidelity, but as a believer, you have a life and understanding that others may lack.

Call to Action: Pay attention to what you have built together, and let go of the past. Remember that with God's help, healing and restoration are possible.

28
CELEBRATING MILESTONES

Two are better than one, because they have a good return for their labor: If either of them falls down, one can help the other up. But pity anyone who falls and has no one to help them up. **Ecclesiastes 4:9**

Celebrating marriage milestones is a significant way to acknowledge and value the journey you have taken together with your spouse. Focusing on the positive things you have created as a team is a lovely way to proceed with building your future together. For example, imagine a 25-year marriage between two people. They may choose to renew their wedding vows, go on vacation together, or host a special dinner for family and friends to mark the occasion. Whatever the celebration may be, it is crucial to recognize the effort and dedication that have gone into the marriage.

As a couple, prioritizing the celebration of marriage milestones is important. Planning and allocating time and resources to commemorate the occasion may be necessary. It is also important to ensure that the values and interests of both partners are reflected in the celebrations, which need not be over-the-top or expensive.

Celebrating milestones in a marriage provides an opportunity to reflect on the journey thus far and to set future goals. Take some time to consider the difficulties you have overcome, the joys you have experienced, and the ways in which you have grown as a couple. Your commitment to each other will grow stronger as a result, and you will be able to appreciate each other more fully.

Call to action: Make celebrating these milestones a regular part of your relationship. Show appreciation for the blessings of your relationship and to appreciate each other more fully.

29
KEEP FINDING JOY AND CONTENTMENT

Rejoice in the Lord always. I will say it again: Rejoice! Let your gentleness be evident to all. ***Philippians 4:4***

A vital component of a fulfilling marriage is finding happiness and contentment together. As a couple, you should intentionally pursue joy and contentment in your marriage. This might mean figuring out what brings happiness to each of you individually and as a couple, and making time to do those things frequently. It may also involve deliberately cultivating an attitude of appreciation and gratitude for one another and focusing on the positive aspects of the relationship.

If you have the opportunity, speak with married couples who have been together for a while. You'll see that many of them faced struggles and difficult times in their marriage. However, they did not give up. They consciously enjoyed being with their partner and were satisfied with the home they created together. It's easy to envy the love and compassion in other people's relationships, but if you take the time to observe, you'll see the effort they put into their relationship.

Decide to continue enjoying and being content in your relationship. Make it a priority to spend time together doing things you both enjoy and showing each other gratitude. Trials and difficulties should not be an excuse to give up on your marriage.

Call to Action: Are you satisfied with your relationship with your spouse? It may be time to consciously invest in your relationship and figure out what makes both of you happy. Avoid comparing your relationship with others and focus on what brings joy to you both individually and as a couple. Remember to prioritize spending time together and expressing gratitude towards each other.

30
THE POWER OF GRATITUDE

Give thanks in all circumstances; for this is God's will for you in Christ Jesus. ***1 Thessalonians 5:18***

Gratitude is a powerful force that can transform all our relationships, including our marriage. The Bible encourages us to count our blessings and give thanks to God for His abundant generosity. In 1 Thessalonians 5:18, it says, "give thanks in all circumstances; for this is the will of God in Christ Jesus for you."

Avoid becoming complacent and taking your spouse for granted. Resist the urge to feel entitled in your relationship. Instead, let your gratitude be reflected in your actions towards your spouse.

Make expressing gratitude a regular part of your marriage. Take the time to reflect on and express gratitude for the different aspects of your relationship. Be intentional about noticing the admirable things that your spouse does and expressing gratitude for those actions.

Acknowledge and appreciate any intentional improvements your spouse makes for the benefit of your relationship. Take the time to discuss it and express gratitude for their efforts.

Make it a practice to thank each other for everything you do, no matter how big or small. Take time to consider and appreciate the blessings in your life.

Gratitude can also be demonstrated through concrete actions, such as showing kindness and thoughtfulness towards your spouse, or simply being there to listen and offer support during difficult times.

Call to Action: By cultivating an attitude of gratitude in your marriage, you can experience a deeper sense of connection, intimacy, and joy. Gratitude can also help to promote forgiveness and reduce feelings of resentment or bitterness.

31
BENEFITS OF SHOWING APPRECIATION

I thank my God every time I remember you. In all my prayers for all of you, I always pray with joy.
Philippians 1:3-4

Building and maintaining healthy relationships, including a happy marriage, depends on mutual appreciation. The Bible emphasizes the significance of expressing gratitude and admiration for other people.

The practice of expressing gratitude should become ingrained in relationships between partners. This may entail expressing appreciation for both significant and insignificant actions taken by your partner, as well as acknowledging the work and sacrifices made in your relationship.

When your spouse gives you a gift or you receive money from your joint savings, try to give your spouse credit for their thoughtfulness. Even if it seems like a small gesture, it's a way of saying "I appreciate you."

Some people consider the things their partners do for them to be their due, and as a result, they don't believe there is a need to express gratitude. But it's important to make it a habit to thank everyone who helps you, including your spouse. Do not take for granted what they are doing for you.

Your partner should feel incredibly fortunate and grateful to have you as a caregiver, and you should also appreciate one another in the relationship. Giving compliments, expressing gratitude for deeds of kindness, and just taking the time to listen and demonstrate empathy when your spouse is going through a trying time are all examples of ways to show appreciation.

Couples who express gratitude to one another in their marriage report feeling more connected and intimate. It can also encourage forgiveness and lessen feelings of bitterness or resentment.

Call to Action: Are you appreciating your spouse enough? Take time today to express your gratitude and appreciation.

32
OVERCOMING BITTERNESS

Get rid of all bitterness, rage, and anger, brawling and slander, along with every form of malice. Be kind and compassionate to one another, forgiving each other, just as in Christ God forgave you. ***Ephesians 4:31-32***

Any marriage can experience feelings of resentment and bitterness, and if they are not addressed, they can lead to irreparable harm. These negative emotions can erode trust over time, damage relationships, and breed more negativity, creating a cycle that is difficult to break. However, with the right attitude, it is possible to overcome bitterness and resentment in your marriage.

First and foremost, it is important to note that Christian couples should strive to avoid experiencing these negative emotions. However, it is possible for a Christian to fall prey to these feelings without a renewed mind. If you find yourself in this situation, the emotions may consume you, and you may become unrecognizable to yourself and your spouse.

If your marriage is struggling with resentment and bitterness, your mental health may be suffering. It's important to pray about it and study God's word. Once you've addressed your mind and made God a priority in your thoughts, you can tackle any other issues related to your mental health.

To overcome resentment and bitterness, it's important to be aware of the problem and act. Be honest with yourself and your spouse about any negative feelings you may be experiencing. Talk about the issue calmly and respectfully, and be open-minded to each other's viewpoints.

The key to overcoming resentment and bitterness is forgiveness. It's crucial to forgive your spouse and let go of any negative feelings that may be hindering your progress.

Call to Action: Instead of dwelling on the negative, try to focus on the good things about your marriage.

33
THE ROLE OF COUNSELING

Without good direction, people lose their way; the wiser counsel you follow, the better your chances. **Proverbs 11:14**

Did you know that the right guidance can help you move and navigate more quickly than you would have otherwise? The right advice can help you make a turn that will keep you from impending problems.

However, I suggest that finding the best advice for your marriage should be your top priority. Seek out those who share your values, as well as those who are Bible scholars and aware of God's teachings.

Your union demands special consideration and tender loving care. There will undoubtedly be obstacles to test what you have built so far. Therefore, during those trying times, seek out people who can provide clarity with God's assistance. Look for counselors who are curious about your life and journey.

Seek the Lord and the appropriate counselors when challenging times arise. Counseling services can be like assistance when encountering a roadblock on a lonely path. If you are surrounded by obstacles and find it challenging to proceed, simply ask for help, and with their support, you can continue traveling towards your destination.

Your choice to seek assistance will save you time and get you back on track rather than forging ahead blindly or putting in a lot of effort to move whatever is hindering your progress.

Call to Action: Do you have a counselor or someone you respect who can advise you when the journey gets tough? Counseling offers a chance for couples to honestly communicate their thoughts and feelings in a safe environment.

34
BUILDING A STRONG MARRIAGE

So they are no longer two, but one flesh. Therefore, what God has joined together, let no one separate. **Matthew 19:6**

The institution of marriage was ordained by God to be an unbroken bond between a man and a woman. As Christians, we all strive for a marriage that lasts a lifetime. However, we see in our world that some marriages come to an end. When issues are left unresolved, some couples may end up getting a divorce.

The fear of failure in your first marriage may linger with you even in subsequent marriages. But I want you to know that you are not a failure. A new relationship can succeed, and you can have a long-lasting companionship. You are not defined by your past. Take some time for yourself and allow God's word to reveal your identity.

When entering a new relationship, it's important to leave any baggage from the past behind and approach it with an open mind. Don't assume that your new partner is like your ex-spouse. You are creating something new together. Place your trust in God and pay attention to building a solid base for your relationship.

Rebuilding a solid marriage after a divorce can be a challenging and difficult journey. But it is possible to have a happy and healthy marriage after going through the trauma and suffering of divorce. Seek healing, let go of the past, communicate clearly, and trust in God's love and grace to aid in the healing process.

Call to Action: Remember that prayer is effective. Share your anxieties and troubles with God. He hears you and will offer you the encouragement and instruction to form a flourishing and lasting marriage.

35
FAMILY DYNAMICS WITH IN-LAWS

Therefore a man shall leave his father and his mother and hold fast to his wife, and they shall become one flesh.
Genesis 2:24 (ESV)

I've heard it said that when you marry someone, you marry their family as well. Depending on how close your spouse is to their family, this statement may or may not be true. The dynamics within the family are also very important.

Even though navigating in-law family dynamics can be difficult, it is crucial to the well-being and success of your marriage. Family members and in-laws frequently bring their own set of standards, viewpoints, and convictions, which can occasionally diverge from your own. But if you have the right attitude and strategy, you can work through these issues and create a solid, happy marriage.

God created the idea of cleaving and departing. Leaving your parents does not imply abandoning them; rather, it means putting your marriage and your partner first. This idea emphasizes how crucial it is to start a new family with your spouse and lay a solid foundation for your union.

Be transparent and truthful with your spouse about your expectations, limitations, and worries regarding family and in-laws. Establish firm boundaries and respectfully discuss them with family members and in-laws. Respect one another's families and traditions while looking for areas of agreement. If necessary, seek the advice of a reputable mediator or counselor.

Remember that your marriage and your spouse should come first. It is important to prioritize your family, but not at the expense of your marriage.

Call to Action: Keep in mind the importance of putting your marriage and your partner first, while still prioritizing your family in a healthy way.

36
SUPPORTING EACH OTHER

May the God who gives endurance and encouragement give you the same attitude of mind toward each other that Christ Jesus had, so that with one mind and one voice you may glorify the God and Father of our Lord Jesus Christ. ***Romans 15:5-6***

Marriage is a journey that has its ups and downs. If life's challenges are not handled carefully, they can damage a marriage. However, couples who support one another through difficult times emerge stronger and more united.

Be present: Be there for your spouse when they are struggling. Actively listen, show empathy, and extend a helping hand. Sometimes, just being there for your partner will make them feel loved and supported.

Pray together: One powerful way to rely on each other and God for strength is to pray together. It can keep you connected and serve as a reminder of your shared faith.

Take care of yourself: During trying times, it's essential to attend to your own physical, emotional, and spiritual needs. This may enable you to support your spouse more effectively.

Don't be afraid to seek help when you need it. This might involve consulting a trustworthy friend, seeking professional counseling, or asking a spiritual guide for guidance.

Encourage one another: When your partner is struggling, offer words of support and remind them of their abilities and strengths. This can uplift their morale and support them in conquering the obstacle.

Call to Action: Are you there for your spouse as you should be? Take a moment to reflect on how you can better support your partner during difficult times.

37
YOUR RELATIONSHIP WITH GOD

Trust in the Lord with all your heart and lean not on your own understanding; in all your ways submit to him, and he will make your paths straight. **Proverbs 3:5-6**

Maintaining a strong relationship with God is not only important for individual spiritual growth but also for the health and longevity of a marriage. Here are some biblical principles and practical ways to ensure God is the cornerstone of your marriage:

Trusting in God means acknowledging that He is the source of wisdom and guidance for our lives, including our marriage. When we submit to Him and seek His will, He can lead us on the right path and help us navigate the ups and downs of married life. Keeping God at the center of your marriage can also help you develop greater love, patience, forgiveness, and compassion towards your spouse.

Think about a triad with God as the leader and you and your spouse as the followers. The more you learn about God, the more intimate you will become to each other. As you both grow in your relationship with God, you will also grow closer together and experience greater intimacy and unity in your marriage.

Take intentional steps to prioritize your relationship with God as a couple. This can include praying together regularly, reading the Bible together, attending church together, and seeking spiritual guidance and support from a pastor or mentor. Make a commitment to trust in God's guidance and to seek His will for your marriage.

By maintaining your relationship with God, you are also investing in the foundation of your marriage and ensuring that it continues to flourish over time. Just as a plant needs regular watering and nourishment to thrive, your marriage needs regular attention and effort to stay strong and healthy.

Call to Action: If you are married, take intentional steps with your spouse to prioritize your relationship with God.

38
SERVING THE LORD TOGETHER

As each one has received a gift, minister it to one another, as good stewards of the manifold grace of God. **1 Peter 4:10**

Working together to serve God's will as a couple can be both fulfilling and rewarding. The Bible teaches that aligning our will with God's will can bring us a greater sense of purpose and joy in life.

In the book of Joshua, God tells Joshua to "be strong and courageous" and to "not be afraid or discouraged" because He will be with him wherever he goes. This key verse emphasizes the importance of relying on God's strength and guidance as we serve Him.

As a couple, it is important to serve one another and to remember that your spouse is both a fellow believer and a fellow soldier for God. Let learning and growth be a regular part of your relationship and community.

Strive to set an example for other believers in your walk with God, honoring Him through your relationship. Let your passion for the Lord shine brightly and impact those around you, fighting for Him together as a team.

Remember that the work we do for God is the only work that matters forever. Stay committed to His will and choose a spouse who is also dedicated to serving Him as your fellow soldier.

Call to Action: Do you see your spouse as a fellow soldier in the Lord's work? Be passionate about serving God together as a couple.

39
ESTABLISHING AN ENDURING MARRIAGE

Husbands, love your wives, just as Christ also loved the church and gave Himself for her. **Ephesians 5:25**

God intended for people to have an everlasting companion when He established the institution of marriage. This union should be treated as a divine, sacred, and holy bond, as described throughout this book, and cherished accordingly by couples.

Just as different materials are used when building a skyscraper versus a bungalow, the question arises: how is your marriage progressing? Are you constructing a relationship that will stand the test of time or one that will crumble after a few years?

According to the Bible, a house is built by wisdom, established by understanding, and furnished with priceless treasures through knowledge. As a person who possesses God's wisdom, you know that a house built on God will not fall.

Therefore, ensure that God is the cornerstone of

your marriage and consciously build upon that foundation. As a team and a couple, carefully consider the construction of your home and be in sync with one another. Prioritizing your relationship with God will have a positive impact on your family, so don't take this lightly. Have constructive, healthy conversations with your spouse and work together to build a lasting home.

Call to Action: Do you want to build a lasting home? Take heed of all that has been said and put God at the center of your relationship. Remember, a house built on God will not fall.

40
LIVING OUT GOD'S PLAN

Have you not read that He who made them (God) made them male and female and said, "This is why a man will leave his father and mother and be joined to his wife, and the two will become one flesh?" They are no longer two, but one body. So, what God has put together, no one should take apart. **Matthew 19:4-6**

When thinking about the idea of marriage, it's important to remember how God created it in the beginning. The idea of marriage comes from the story of how God made man and how Adam and Eve got married. This view stresses that marriage is not just a human plan, but also a divine institution.

As Christians, we have a duty to protect the purity of marriage because it is a promise made by God. They represent God's plan for peace, love, and unity when a man and a woman get married.

How we act and think about marriage should show that we know what God wants for us. We are to show love and unity among ourselves, just like Christ did with the church. God planned for marriage to be a lifelong relationship in which both partners count on God for support and provision and help each other, share secrets, and be friends. For a marriage to work, both people must live by the ideals of love, devotion, and selflessness.

Call to Action: If you haven't been honoring your marriage as much as you should, remember that God created it to be holy. Protect its holiness and make a promise to follow the rules that make a marriage work.

Connect with Ben Seyi-Ola
by scanning the QR code below

Other Books By Ben Seyi-Ola

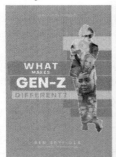

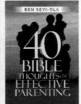
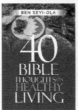

Made in the USA
Middletown, DE
04 March 2024